Classic Sports Cars

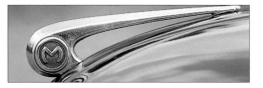

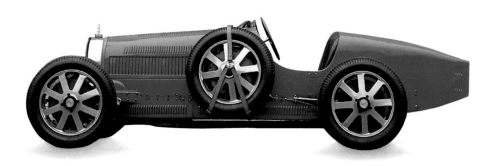

Classic Sports Cars

A marque-by-marque guide
to over 35 dream cars

Iain Ayre

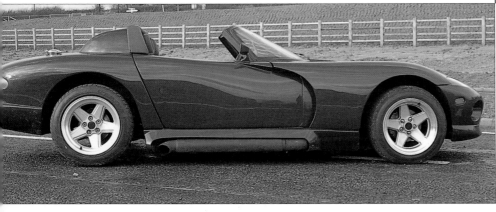

LORENZ BOOKS

This edition is published by Lorenz Books

Lorenz Books is an imprint of Anness Publishing Ltd
Hermes House, 88–89 Blackfriars Road, London SE1 8HA
tel. 020 7401 2077; fax 020 7633 9499
www.lorenzbooks.com; info@anness.com

This edition distributed in the UK by The Manning Partnership Ltd, 6
The Old Dairy, Melcombe Road, Bath BA2 3LR; tel. 01225 478 444;
fax 01225 478 440; sales@manning-partnership.co.uk

This edition distributed in the USA and Canada by National Book Network,
4501 Forbes Boulevard, Suite 200, Lanham, MD 20706; tel. 301 459 3366;
fax 301 429 5746; www.nbnbooks.com

This edition distributed in Australia by Pan Macmillan Australia, Level 18,
St Martins Tower, 31 Market St, Sydney, NSW 2000; tel. 1300 135 113;
fax 1300 135 103; customer.service@macmillan.com.au

A CIP catalogue record for this book is available from the British Library.

Publisher: Joanna Lorenz
Senior Editor: Alison Macfarlane
Designer: Lisa Tai

Previously published as Sports Car Classics

10 9 8 7 6 5 4 3 2 1

CONTENTS

The first sports car came only a few years after the first motor car. Its origins are as obvious as its existence was inevitable. The first step was to clamber aboard a wheezing, oily veteran, which was then the latest and most exotic technological toy, and to feel the excitement of controlling it, rumbling along a dirt road under its own power. The second step was to wonder about stripping it down to a bare chassis with just a couple of bucket seats, to make it go a bit faster. Thus was the sports car born.

The 1905 Gordon Bennett Trials on the Isle of Man saw the Hon. Charles Rolls doing 60mph (96kph) in his Wolseley, trailing a huge cloud of dust and enjoying exactly the same sensations that enthusiastic drivers have enjoyed ever since – and 60mph in a 1905 Wolseley on dirt roads must have been a whole lot of fun. That

Below: **The 1905 Gordon Bennett Cup, held in Auvergne, France, sees Mr C. Bianchi in his Wolseley. There is something delightful in the knowledge that Wolseley, one of Britain's most respected car makers over 80 years, started out making sheep shearing machinery! Many a sheep has been shorn since the Wolseley company was born, in 1896.**

6

INTRODUCTION

wasn't the fastest entry. The Napier L-43, with radiator tubing running all across the front and sides of the bonnet to aid cooling, was capable of 105mph (168kph) and had briefly held the World Land Speed Record.

Ettore Bugatti was involved in the same sort of games, and a recent delightful find was his own 1915 racer, which has been lovingly looked after by a restorer and is still used, and used hard, in classic trials. However, after each outing, the cylinder block is now X-rayed, as a rod through the side of that particular engine would have to be the most expensive automotive bang you could ever hear.

The world of sports cars remained pretty exclusive as the years went by. In fact, hardly anybody even had a car, never mind a sports car. The sporting Bentleys described by Ettore Bugatti as the fastest lorries in the world would have cost

Above: **The 45 hp Napier prepares to do battle in the 1903 Gordon Bennett race. The year before, the famous racing cyclist Selwyn Francis Edge had won the annual event in a four-cylinder 30 hp Napier.**

Below: **Frank Clement and Chassagne in a 1929 4½ litre Le Mans Bentley. In that year at the celebrated French 24-hour race, the Bentleys swept aside the Chryslers and Stutzes to take the first four places with ease.**

more or less the same in real terms in 1929 as the equivalent Bentley costs now, and they are of course hugely expensive. (They still weigh about the same, too.)

The Italians have always had a fascination with sports cars, and the Maserati company's chequered history exemplifies the history of the upmarket sports car manufacturer. The company started off with light, beautifully engineered racing cars, in 1926. Financially bereft of any serious backing, Maserati produced two of the all-time great racing cars, in the days when talent and imagination rather than

Below and underneath: **Maserati's 250F has to be one of the most pleasing shapes of any racing car. The driver sits on it rather than in it. From the first Maserati of 1926 to that of the late 1940s virtually all of the company's cars were strictly racing models. The Neptune's trident badge the company adopted is that of the city of Bologna.**

budgets and marketing deals were more important. Their 250F is a sublime shape, and their Birdcage chassis was a wonderful blend of art and engineering. To stay at the front of the GP grids, and to stay in business, they clothed some of their racing chassis in roadgoing bodywork, producing some of the purest sports cars ever. In 1956, they recorded their highest ever annual production figure: 34!

Ferrari and Lamborghini also kept the Italian line going, as more purpose-built sports cars began to emerge.

However, for every exclusive thoroughbred sports racer, there are hundreds of more humble sports cars, which have given their owners ninety per cent of the pleasures of fast, open air motoring for ten per cent of the cost of a "serious" car. The tradition of stripping down ordinary cars to lose weight, then beefing up the engine, is well illustrated by the Model T. A few years after the Model T was launched, cut-down performance versions were being cooked up in backyards all over America, with upside-down axles, single-seater aluminium bodies, overhead cam conversions and limited-slip differentials. Interestingly, lots of these Model T conversions were capable of speeds in excess of 100mph (160kph), so there has been surprisingly little progress since, in terms of sheer speed.

On both sides of the Atlantic as the century wore on, the idea of what the term "sports car" should signify evolved to mean fairly humble mechanical components in a pretty, usually convertible body. In the States this means something rather different than in Europe. The early Corvettes, Mustangs and Thunderbirds may have had "cooking" engines fitted (i.e. nothing out of the ordinary), but an ordinary 6 litre V8, even in standard trim, is capable of some serious acceleration. The European alternative approach eschewed power and performance, and went for charm instead. Morris Garages modified family Morrises to create the early MGs, which puttered about with tiny engines and skinny wheels. They didn't go anywhere very fast, but they went there with style.

Above: **"MG"** originally signified one more carburettor than normal and a sports body. The MGTF (1953), the last of the old MG Midgets, carried on the tradition: pretty, amusing but very slow. One American journalist described it as a "dead cat slightly warmed over."

Below: **MG** sports cars have provided the public with low-budget fun cars since before the Second World War.

The illustrious names of Talbot and Sunbeam were co-opted for quite a pretty but otherwise unremarkable 1950s sports tourer, to considerable grumbling from enthusiasts. When the same names were again taken in vain and put on a really horrible Rootes shopper of the 1980s, the grumbling got worse.

Sports cars have always attracted strong and loyal followings, and some of them both in the UK and the US have enjoyed remarkably long production runs, provided the manufacturers have had the sense to keep to the point and give the buyers what they want. The Chevrolet Corvette, although mutating into a variety of different shapes through the last 40 years or so, has kept the faith, and is still a fast, sexy car, with lots of raw power and

Above: **The TR5 is for many people the best of the TRs. Leather, walnut and a baritone exhaust bark. A conservative approach was always part of the original Triumph makeup: having been successful with motorcycles they were late to enter into the car market – 1923.**

Above: **The TR3A evolved from the basic TR2. With a little more comfort and a chrome-plated grin at the front, this was an attractive car. It helped to extend the TR dynasty: TR2, 3, and TR3A sold 83,000 units up to 1962.**

spectacular two-seater bodywork in GRP. The 1997 Corvette is sleeker and more sophisticated than the 1955 car, but it still fits the definition of a Corvette.

Triumph were going strong with the TR series until things went horribly wrong in the 1970s. The first TRs were very open, basic sports cars, with strong but crude four-cylinder engines developed from a tractor power unit. They had hefty brakes and steering that was also reminiscent of a tractor. However, they were attractive, in a stumpy, frog-eyed way, and their basic proportions were good. They were also fun to drive, with cutaway doors and a low stance. The TR series carried on through TR2, 3, and 3A with similar styling, then an Italian rework by Michelotti brought the car up to date without spoiling its character. The six-cylinder engine from the contemporary Triumph saloon powered up the performance, and a very clean redesign by Karmann again preserved the basic good looks

of the car and sharpened it up for the early 1970s. The TR7 stopped the TR series dead. Deeply ugly, it lost the separate chassis, the six-cylinder engine, the convertible roof, the stiff handling, in fact everything that made the TRs sports cars. It was a short, nasty saloon car, only fit for shopping, and not even much use for that, with dubious build quality and two seats missing.

The present climate, however, is set fair for sports cars. The fear of convertibles being legislated out of existence has receded. The 1980s were almost completely devoid of proper sports cars, the only alternative being hot hatchbacks. Very sensible, but if there's room for a baby seat, then for some it just isn't a sports car.

Above: **The end of an era. The ugly wedge-shaped TR7 spelled the demise of the Triumph name for most enthusiasts. With a soft top and a V8 engine fitted in 1980 it was better, but not much. With the last TR7s rolled out in 1981, owners British Leyland sold off the Liverpool factory.**

11

While the Triumph name has for the moment been allowed to die off with dignity, the MGF carries on the name in a car which is actually rather too pure a sports car to be regarded as a proper MG. The genuine MG tradition means humble shopping saloons modified slightly in early cars (extra carb, MG badge, little else) or more radically modified saloon mechanicals as in the MGB (Austin Cambridge, sports body, extra carb, that's it). The rear mid-engined MGF is an advanced dedicated design, owing little to the parts-bin tradition of MG.

Left: **The small company of TVR carries the tradition of British sports cars into the 1990s with pretty and explosively fast V8s. The look of the these cars certainly belies the affordable price.**

Above: **The 1990s MGF is an ultra-modern mid-engined car, and represents a worthy new direction for the celebrated MG name. Though there are question marks about the "chunky" styling. It's not Italian, for sure.**

TVR's current run of success is also encouraging – two seats, V8 power, GRP bodies and straightforward backbone steel chassis welded together in Blackpool. While TVR have left their kit car origins behind, only retaining the healthy traditions of strong chassis and radical GRP bodies, the kit car industry in both the UK and the US is progressing in leaps and bounds, producing some quite astonishingly innovative designs and displaying high standards of manufacture – and what's more, quite often for only a small percentage of the cost of production cars.

Any selection of sports cars is bound to leave out many examples whose omission will baffle and enrage enthusiasts. There is no definitive list of best sports cars – this book simply features a selection of European and American sports cars that have special appeal.

BUYING A CLASSIC CAR

Yachting has been tellingly compared with standing in a cold shower tearing up money, and classic cars are no different – coming up with large amounts of money to stop them falling apart is also a feature of the hobby. However, yachties and classic car buffs seem to keep coming back for more, so there must be something in it.

For the inexperienced, buying a classic car can be a minefield. An intelligent first move is to pick a marque you fancy, join the club, go along to meetings and listen. You will find out where the best cars are, you will find out what design faults all the owners are now having to deal with, and you will get endless and enthusiastic help when it comes to hunting down a car and then keeping it going.

Going off on your own and learning the hard way also has its positive points, though. The trick is to start off with something affordable, and to learn from your mistakes. Don't start with a Mercedes that looks quite shiny apart from a few rust bubbles: you would not believe what spare parts for a Mercedes cost. How about £1,600 ($1,000) for a bumper?

If you buy an old Triumph Spitfire, on the other hand, there is a huge and thriving club devoted to supplying you with cheap parts and lots of help. When you buy your first Spitfire and drive it home, you will enjoy it enormously, although you will listen for peculiar noises immediately. This is one difference between classic and ordinary motoring – a Datsun will give 200,000 miles (320,000 kilometres) of boring motoring without breaking down, the Triumph will not. The back end, for instance, is poorly designed and not necessarily well put together, and Spitfire owners spend their time

Above: **The most obvious advice is almost always the best, and the hardest to follow: when you go to an auction, decide on your price limit and stick with it, despite the temptation to keep bidding.**

Above: **Some fabulous exotica turn up at auctions, sometimes apparently being knocked down remarkably cheaply. Leave them to the experts until you know what you're doing, and if you are not to be dissuaded, consult the owners' club beforehand.**

listening for new noises from behind. When you investigate underneath in response to a new grumble, you will realize just what a state the body and chassis are in, and then the fun really starts. This is one benefit of running replicas – their bodies and chassis will generally stay solid indefinitely.

However, classic cars are essentially very repairable, unlike modern cars. A failed ECU on a BMW will probably cost rather more than a completely rebuilt engine for a Spitfire, and you can rebuild a Spitfire engine in your garage.

When choosing a marque, unless you have any preferences, give old Fords a thought. Because of misplaced snobbery, they are very undervalued, and you can pick

Above: **MG sports cars tend to be firm in the market. There aren't many bargains to be had, but parts are in good supply and running costs are cheap. As always, it is a tricky trade-off between price and running costs.**

Above: **Has someone bought a bargain or a "lemon"? They will find out soon enough. The thrill of the chase is quite intoxicating at auctions, so beware.**

up some astonishing bargains that would be four times the price if they had an MG badge on their bonnets.

Buying at auction is exciting, but there is a strong temptation to get carried away, and some of the worst examples of classic cars can appear at auction. It's best to leave auctions until you can tell filler from steel, and until you know a lot about your chosen marque.

After a year or two of keeping a cheap classic on the road, your toolbox and confidence will be full, and you can sell your first classic – for a profit, with a bit of luck – and progress to something more ambitious.

Best of luck, and see you in a year or two at Goodwood – the biggest classic car event in the world.

AC COBRA

In its day the fastest production car in the world, the AC Cobra was the result of some imagination and fast talking by one Carroll Shelby, an American race driver who had been sidelined by heart problems. As he couldn't drive on the track at maniac speeds any more, he decided to build cars that would do it in his name, and his approach was to combine the best that both British and American engineering could produce.

An example of all that is best about British sports cars was the AC Ace, a genuinely beautiful, lightweight two-seater, with a strong ladder chassis and a delicate tracery of tubing supporting a handmade aluminium body. The engine was a jewel of a six-cylinder two-litre by Bristol, but Bristol stopped making it, leaving AC in real trouble: they tried Ford Zephyr engines, but without much success. Then Shelby came along and told them that he was backed by Ford and wanted to shoehorn the new small-block 260 V8 into an AC. Great, said AC. Shelby then went to Ford, told them he was backed by AC and got them involved as well. The result was the Cobra. They are not really as fearsome to drive as they are some-

Right: **The size of tyres necessary to keep a grip on the track meant huge wheel arches bulging out the sides of the car in the ultimate 427 SC version. For lovers of speed, this was a marriage made in heaven.**

16

Right: **Initially the Cobra still looked like an Ace, but the engine sizes went up from 5 litres to 7.5, and the body had to change.**

AC COBRA 1962–68

⊛ **BODY/CHASSIS** Ladder chassis with two main 4in/10cm (later 5in/12.5cm) round-tube chassis beams and smaller section upper structures. Body: unstressed aluminium on Superleggera-style frame.

⊛ **ENGINE** Initially 260cu in Ford cast iron small-block V8; latterly 289 and 427 big-block, with additional tuning options, front-mounted and longitudinal.

⊛ **TRANSMISSION** Four-speed Ford manual gearbox, fixed rear diff.

⊛ **SUSPENSION** Initially, independent by transverse leaf springs. Later, coils and wishbones.

times made out to be, but if you are rough or overconfident on the track, the chassis starts to flex a little and you are suddenly in more trouble than most people have the skill or reflexes to get out of.

The Cobra represented Shelby's approach to life in general – "Too much is just right." Whether or not you think it's the most charismatic car in the world, the AC Cobra is probably the most replicated car ever. There are more replicas on the road today than there ever were real Cobras; in the US replica market, the Cobra totally dominates.

Below: **The 427 has the reputation of being an absolute animal, but this is mostly speculation. Driven smoothly and well, a Cobra can still leave a lot of very quick cars eating its dust – on or off the track.**

AUBURN 851 SPEEDSTER

Styled by Gordon Buehrig of Cord fame, the US Auburn Speedster was the last in the line of Auburn cars. By the early 1920s, the Auburn concern was in bad shape, and its acquisition by Cord gave it a new lease of life. Over the next 10 years, Auburns featured some increasingly spectacular body styles and a series of Lycoming engines. Auburns were all fast, and all stylish. The 851 ran a Lycoming flathead straight eight, with a three-speed gearbox that was effectively turned into a six-speed by the inclusion of a two-speed rear axle, with ratios of 3.0:1 and 4.5:1.

The bodywork was fantastic and modernistic, with an even more absurd ratio of body size to usable interior space than a Jaguar XK120. The running boards are irresistibly Chicago, but this was a lot sleeker than most of the Roaring Twenties gangster transport. There wasn't room for any more than two people, but at least one Auburn had a little door cut in the side allowing access to a long, thin compartment running right across the car behind the seat: this was intended for the owner's golf clubs.

The 4.5 litre engine was available in either supercharged or normally aspirated form, so the performance to some extent matched the bodywork, at least in a straight line. It's a shame that Auburn didn't survive. What would their new model have looked like?

AUBURN 851 SPEEDSTER 1931–37

BODY/CHASSIS Twin rail ladder chassis with cross bracing. Two-door convertible bodywork in steel.

ENGINE Front mounted longitudinal flathead sidevalve straight eight, alloy cylinder head, 280cu in/4585cc.

Stromberg carb, Schweitzer-Cummins supercharger.

TRANSMISSION Three-speed manual with two-speed rear axle.

SUSPENSION Front beam axle, rear live axle, both on semi-elliptic springs with lever arm shocks.

18

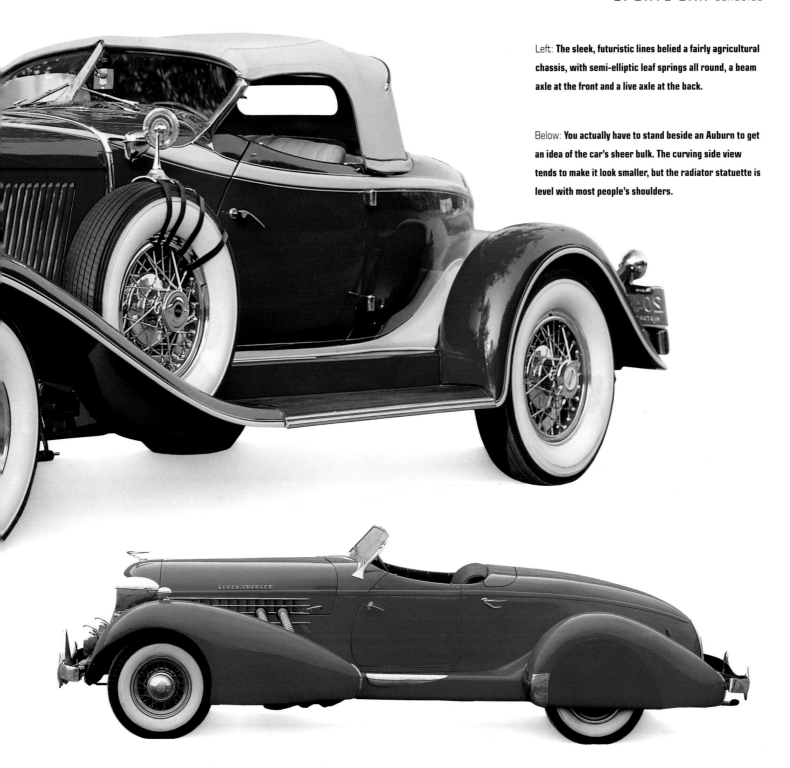

Left: **The sleek, futuristic lines belied a fairly agricultural chassis, with semi-elliptic leaf springs all round, a beam axle at the front and a live axle at the back.**

Below: **You actually have to stand beside an Auburn to get an idea of the car's sheer bulk. The curving side view tends to make it look smaller, but the radiator statuette is level with most people's shoulders.**

19

AUSTIN-HEALEY

The origins of the Austin-Healey lie in the friendship of Donald Healey and Leonard Lord of Austin. The bloated Austin Atlantic had been a failure, but its engine and underpinnings had proved stout and reliable.

Healey took the engine and built a chassis around it which was tough enough to take the considerable weight of the Atlantic engine, but still light enough to provide a reasonable turn of speed. The car was intended to take the slice of the market between the Jaguar XK120 and the MGA, and shared some of the styling themes of both, but added its own bullish charm.

The car was an immediate success, and won the New York Motor Show's Car of the Year award in 1952. Car of the Year really

AUSTIN-HEALEY 1952–67

⚘ **BODY/CHASSIS** Ladder chassis with cross bracing. Steel two-door convertible bodywork.

⚘ **ENGINE** Originally four-cylinder, cast iron 2660cc Austin engine; later, straight six of 2990cc.

⚘ **TRANSMISSION** Originally three-speed with overdrive, later four-speed with overdrive. Live rear axle.

⚘ **SUSPENSION** Front: double wishbones with coil springs and lever arm shocks. Rear: leaf springs, lever arm shocks, Panhard rod.

Above: **The Healey's engine had been developed from a pre-war six-cylinder light truck engine, and later saw service in the Champ Jeep in four-cylinder form.**

meant something then, before it began to be awarded to inadequate shopping hatchbacks. Prizes aside, the 3,000 orders taken at the launch of the car were also significant, and Austin geared up to full production as quickly as Jaguar had tooled up for the XK120, and for the same reason.

In 3000 form, the car became more of a grand tourer, and although the steering and the other controls were still heavy, there was so much torque that you didn't really need to change gear very much – once in top, you could stay there as long as you liked.

Right: **A lightweight version of the Austin-Healey won Sebring in first, second and third place at Le Mans in 1955, pushing Jaguars and Ferraris out of the way, and earned itself a place in motoring history.**

Left: **Nearly all sporting cars get older and fatter as they evolve, and the next generation of Healeys were fitted with the engine from the Austin Westminster, a six-cylinder, 3 litre version of the old truck engine.**

21

HUMBLE ORIGINS

●●●

TRIUMPH **SPITFIRE**
TRIUMPH **HERALD**
MG **MIDGET**
MG **MORRIS MINOR**

Some of our best-loved sports cars have come from humble origins, and most enthusiasts are quite happy with that. A sports car is not necessarily about speed, after all – it's more a question of style and flavour.

The Triumph Spitfire, one of Michelotti's prettier designs for Triumph, is more or less the same car as the Triumph Herald. A great number of the parts are interchangeable, and the chassis itself only differs in its proportions.

Also shared are the suspension and handling characteristics, including the excellent front end with its double wishbones and its extremely tight turning circle, and the fairly awful swing arm back end, with its tendency to jack up the rear on to one sidewall halfway round a corner. This doesn't happen quite as often as some people would like to have us believe but it is extremely unpleasant when it does.

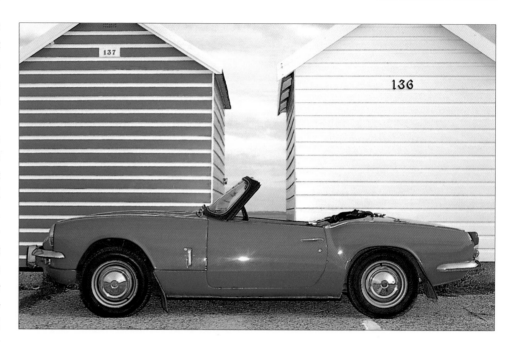

Left and above: **The Spitfire and Herald were built concurrently and shared more or less the same chassis. This was possible partly because the company couldn't build its own bodies originally, which meant bolt-on panels.**

Above and below: **Despite being a rebodied Herald, the Spitfire had a completely different feel and was tremendously entertaining to drive. The coupé version would emerge as the GT6.**

Spitfire and Herald engines and gearboxes are interchangeable, and many of the twin-carb set-ups originally on Spitfires have found their way on to Heralds. The ultimate small sports Triumph was the GT6, which took the Spitfire body, turned it into a coupé and put it on a 2 litre-engined Vitesse chassis.

The MG Midget is another perennially popular small sports car, and was the main competition for the Spitfire. The Spitfire was faster, roomier and more comfortable, but the Midget, which was also marketed as the Austin-Healey Sprite, handled better.

The MG Midget was essentially a rebodied Morris Minor, and it also shared

Above left: **The MG Midget (shown here) and Austin-Healey Sprite shared the Morris Minor engine.**

Above right: **The Morris Minor itself is a timeless classic in its own right, but it's no sports car!**

many of its mechanicals with the earlier Austin A30. The same familiar A-series engine, in transverse form, powered the Mini. Early Sprites and Midgets started off with small versions of the A-series, and gradually they got bigger until the later Midgets were powered by a Morris Marina-sourced 1500cc straight four, using a gearbox shared with the Spitfire; it had

finally occurred to someone within the company, which sold both Spridgets and Spitfires, that there was very little point in competing against themselves in parts supply as well as in the market place.

This tradition of MG providing sporting versions of their run-of-the-mill shopping cars goes back now for about 60 years: the least convincing example was the MG-badged Morris 1100 of the early 1960s. There are occasional exceptions, such as the sublime supercharged six-cylinder sports cars of the 1930s and the current MGF, both of which are serious performance cars rather than traditional MG sports cars.

BENTLEY LE MANS

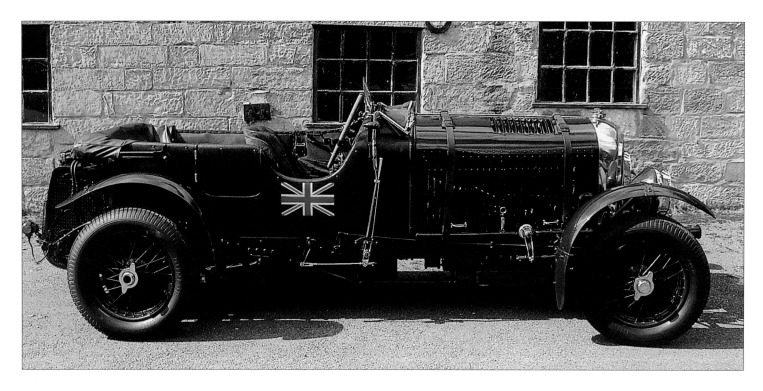

The supercharged UK "4½ litre" Blower Bentleys are arguably the most charismatic cars that were ever built. W.O. Bentley was among the first, if not *the* first, to use aluminium pistons, and the specifications of his engines were remarkably "modern": overhead camshafts, four valves per cylinder and twin plug ignition. Oddly enough, twin spark plugs have been enjoying a revival, for the same reason that they were used before World War II – poor quality petrol. W.O. Bentley did not approve of

Above: **The Le Mans Bentleys were in no sense pure racing cars – they still had four genuine seats – and they won with a blend of horsepower and staying power which gave birth to the legend of the racing "Bentley Boys."**

supercharging, and it seems that once the engine had been modified to suit superchargers, the power was more or less the same as the Le Mans-winning Speed Sixes, which didn't have superchargers. The same amount of power achieved with the addition of complicated machinery did not seem to represent progress, as far as W.O. was concerned.

However, the Amherst-Villiers supercharger's aluminium casing protruding through the classically elegant Bentley grille really says it all, as far as classic sports cars go.

Left: **The dashboard looks haphazard, but everything is where it is for a reason, with the rev counter taking pride of place.**

BENTLEY LE MANS 1923–31

⚙ **BODY/CHASSIS** Twin rail ladder chassis, cross-braced, with coachbuilt ash/ horsehair/fabric and aluminium bodywork.

⚙ **ENGINE** Four-cylinder, cast iron monobloc, 4398cc, single overhead camshaft, four valves per cylinder, two SU carburettors pressurized by Amherst-Villiers supercharger, twin magnetos and coils.

⚙ **TRANSMISSION** Single dry plate clutch, separate four-speed crash gearbox, live rear axle.

⚙ **SUSPENSION** Front: beam axle, leaf springs, friction dampers. Rear: live axle, leaf springs, friction dampers.

Reliability was very important for Bentley. For example, the reason for avoiding detachable cylinder heads was the generic unreliability of head gaskets. Likewise, overhead cams and four valves per cylinder meant lighter and less stressed valve trains.

A vintage Bentley will accelerate smoothly from 5mph (8kph) to over 120mph (192kph) in top gear, and there aren't many modern cars that could do that. Changing gear is something to be avoided: it takes years of practice to avoid crunching the cogs.

25

Above: **Ettore Bugatti famously described the Bentleys as the fastest lorries in the world. But only because they beat him. By 1928, however, when this picture was taken, W.O. was aware that the progressive weight increase in the Bentleys was a serious problem.**

Above: **It's worth inspecting an early Bentley carefully, as the quality of the engineering and finish really is exquisite. The number of cars produced by Bentley is remarkably high in comparison with, say, Aston Martin, in the same period.**

BUGATTI TYPE 35

The debut of the Italian Type 35 Bugatti was at the 1924 French Grand Prix. This was the first time Ettore Bugatti's talents had really come together in one car, and the Type 35 proved to be an extremely successful racing car over the next five or six years, before the engine design was overtaken by others. It was also a very successful privateer sports racer at club level, with many exclusive racing series run for and by the *Bugattisti*.

The shape and proportions of the Type 35 were sublime, and followed Bugatti's twin preoccupations of art and engineering. The horseshoe radiator set the shape for the front of the car, and the body stayed lithe and minimal past the narrow cockpit to the delicate, tapered tail.

It's always a surprise to find out just how tiny a Type 35 is. The car is really a single seater, with a little perch for a mechanic off to one side. The elegant cast aluminium wheels were not only intended to save weight: they also saved money, as hand-built wire wheels were no cheaper then than they are now. The engine revved to 5,500 rpm, which by the standards of the day was pretty astonishing – most people were relying on huge engines that would only reach about half that number of revs.

Above: **Exquisite machine turning on the dash is typical of the high quality of Bugatti detailing.**

Right: **Many Type 35s were used by private owners for road and week-end racing use.**

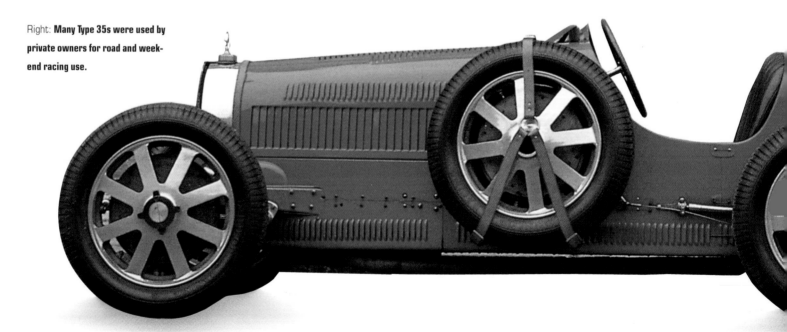

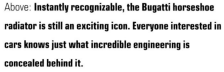

Above: **Instantly recognizable, the Bugatti horseshoe radiator is still an exciting icon. Everyone interested in cars knows just what incredible engineering is concealed behind it.**

Above: **If you were entering the Targa Florio at any time between 1925 and 1929, there was little point in turning up without a Type 35.**

Right: **2 litres, straight eight. Capable of revving to unheard of numbers.**

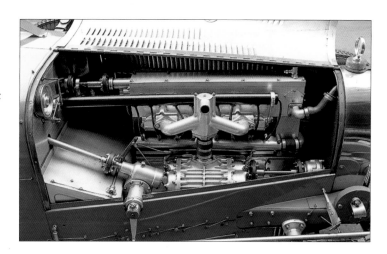

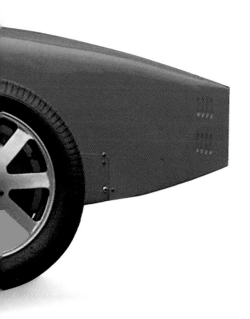

BUGATTI TYPE 35 1924–29

🜔 **BODY/CHASSIS** Twin rail ladder chassis, open road/racing body in aluminium.

🜔 **ENGINE** 1995cc straight eight double monobloc, roller bearing crank. Overhead cam, 3 valves per cylinder, Zenith/Solex carburettor, later supercharged.

🜔 **TRANSMISSION** Multiplate wet clutch, separate four-speed crash box, live axle.

🜔 **SUSPENSION** Front: hollow beam axle on leaf springs, friction dampers. Rear: quarter elliptic springs, friction dampers.

CHEVROLET CORVETTE STING RAY

The concept behind the US Corvette was down to two men – Harley Earl, who wanted to make a small, sleek sports car as good as the European sports cars he had always admired, and Chevrolet's chief engineer Ed Cole, who thought a flagship sports car would do Chevrolet's staid image no harm at all.

The car's underpinnings were developed by Robert MacLean and Maurice Olley, who worked towards a 50/50 weight distribution and a low centre of gravity.

Although the handling of the original Corvette was not at all sophisticated, it was acceptable for 1953. Chevrolet have remained remarkably loyal to the original

concept and current models of the car are still based on a steel chassis with a glass fibre body. Today's cars are immensely powerful, despite emissions limitations, and the suspension has developed through several decades of progress in design.

In the late 1960s, the thunderclouds of emission controls were still gathering, and

Left: The 1968 Corvette Sting Ray is a very pure example of the breed. The chassis still looks like that of a farm trailer, but the body, inspired by the 1965 Mako Shark II show car, is a gorgeous blend of razor-edge styling and muscular curves. The needle nose is defined by a thin strip of chrome bumper, the front is uncluttered by headlights and the wheel arches front and rear bulge out from a narrow, sculptured waist.

Above: From 1965, the Corvette had been fitted with disc brakes all round, which was something of a comfort given the engine size, but the handling was still compromised by the paramount importance of ride comfort across the expanses of long, straight American roads.

CHEVROLET CORVETTE STING RAY 1953–

⊛ **CHASSIS/BODY** Chassis: pressed steel box section ladderframe, with X bracing. Body: unstressed GRP shell, convertible or coupé.

⊛ **ENGINE** Front-mounted longitudinal cast iron V8 with cast iron heads. Single cams in block, pushrods, hydraulic tappets.

⊛ **TRANSMISSION** Three- or four-speed manual, or three-speed Powerglide automatic.

⊛ **SUSPENSION** Independent all round, with double unequal length wishbones and coil springs in front and transverse leaf springs at the rear.

the engine options available for the Corvette included the 427 cubic inch (7 litre) big-block V8, on four-barrel carbs. In a relatively light GRP-bodied car, the acceleration was breathtaking, and with fuel still measured in cents rather than dollars, the car's ravenous consumption of fuel was not a handicap. Handling was still not sophisticated – but by the time you have admired a 1968 Sting Ray, looked down the endless curves of the bonnet, felt the torque and listened to the rumble of a big-block, who cares how it handles? The Corvette story is far from over; these days, it's still a sports car, unlike so many other great names of the past, misused on drab machinery.

CLASSIC REPLICAS

The replica phenomenon has grown and developed with the kit car industry over the last 20 years or so. Many of the less accomplished replicas and kits have fallen by the wayside, leaving some excellent and well-developed cars to be enjoyed by those in the know.

The reasons why people build or buy replicas are as individual as people themselves, but are largely down to the prices and the value of the real cars. For example, you may not be able to afford a genuine 427 Cobra. However, there is an entire industry devoted to replicating the Cobra, with 50 or so companies competing for business worldwide. The basic package from the UK-based Pilgrim company represents the more down-to-earth affordable Cobra replica, and their kit can be bought in its simplest form for as little as £3,000 ($4,500).

If you build a Cobra for that sort of money, it will look like it. However, if you put in a sensible amount of time and money, and use the lightweight Rover V8, the result will look like a genuine Cobra, and will even sound fairly convincing. It won't be anywhere near as awesome as the real thing, but a lot of people have had a lot of driving satisfaction out of low-budget Cobra replicas.

The motivation for building replicas can be a mix of practicality and respect for the historical importance of the real thing. You may not be able buy a new one because production has ceased and a genuine old car, although still fast and beautiful, is often elderly, fragile and valuable both in terms of money and historical importance. With such classics, the best option is a good-

Above: **The Allard, replicated with the help of a massive V12 Jaguar engine, captures the spirit of the original. In 1952, Sydney Allard won the Monte Carlo Rally in one of his own cars (a P-Type saloon), a feat never repeated.**

Left: **Is this the real Dodge Viper? Not at $18,000 (£12,000). But this replica does run a 427CI V8, so it is most certainly in the right mood.**

quality replica which will look just as beautiful as the original. The Jaguar XK120 replica, for example, has been moulded from a real Jaguar but the mechanicals are from a recycled Series II Jaguar XK6, which still runs the same engine as the first XK120s. A good XJ6-based replica is much stronger and faster, handles better and the brakes are huge four-pot vented discs.

As far as classic Jaguars go, all the best ones are available in replica form – the SS100, the XK120, the D-type, the C-Type and even the E-type, although you could buy a real E-Type for the cost of building a

Above left: **This budget Cobra replica from British firm Pilgrim costs about £4,000 ($6,200). Double the price and you build a great-looking car with a Rover V8 engine.**

Above right: **You would never guess, at least from a distance, and if you didn't look inside and weren't a diehard *tifosi*, that this is not a Ferrari. It is actually a Pontiac Fiero with a factory body kit.**

replica. On the other hand the replica is still a Jaguar, looks identical to the real thing, is ten times as strong and will never rust, so perhaps it is worth thinking about.

One interesting tale is that of General Motors' Pontiac Fiero. The Fiero looks remarkably like the Ferrari 308 – so much so that the British kit car company, The Fiero Factory, is able to make a close replica of the 308 simply by changing the outer body panels.

Another interesting and successful replica is the British/Canadian Allard, built in tiny numbers in an old dairy in rural Hertfordshire, England. The prototype runs a Jaguar V12 with a forest of Webers and is as fast as it is ugly, although it is also loaded with charm and beautifully built.

Right: **One of the author's own Ayrspeed Six XK120 replicas. The donor car is the Jaguar XJ6.**

31

CHEVROLET CAMARO

The Mustang phenomenon led the way for the other major American car manufacturers, and the Camaro was General Motors' version. Like the Ford, there was a very basic version of the car sporting a relatively feeble straight six, but the options were endless. The bottom level V8 was the small-block 5 litre 327CI, and the top powerplant available for the road-going Camaro, in the SS model, was the 210 bhp 350CI V8. The name Camaro in Spanish can mean "upset stomach," and with 375 bhp and a live axle on leaf springs, the name seems unusually apt.

The Camaro is one of the most handsome American cars ever and hangs together so well as a design that you do not notice how extreme some of the features are until you really look closely. The relationship of the very small coupé rear side windows to the very big hump of the rear wing really shouldn't work, but somehow it does; and beautifully. Even the convertible looks good, with the styling of the top following the original roofline very closely.

CHEVROLET CAMARO 1966–

⚙ **CHASSIS/BODY** Monocoque coupé and convertible bodies with front subframe structure.

⚙ **ENGINE** Front mounted longitudinal cast iron straight sixes or V8s in 327cu in, 350cu in and 396cu in sizes.

⚙ **TRANSMISSION** Three-/four-speed manual, or two-/three-speed automatic.

⚙ **SUSPENSION** Front: double wishbones with coil-over shocks. Rear: live axle on leaf springs.

Above: **There was a Camaro called the Z28, which was developed for racing and was technically also a road car. But with a 396CI engine producing 375 bhp, you wouldn't have seen many of those parked outside the "Piggly Wiggly" supermarket.**

Left: **The chassis of the Camaro differed from the Mustang in that rather than a straightforward monocoque, the Camaro featured a shell with a large front subframe, allowing considerable improvements in ride comfort and noise levels, but at the expense of handling on the limit.**

Above: **The interior of the Camaro copied the Mustang, with a similar, vast range of options on offer. At the time of the Camaro's introduction, Chevrolet were on a high; they passed the 50-million car mark a few years before.**

Below: **Camaros are great to watch competing side-by-side with Mustangs on the track. Camaro has more power, but the Mustang handles better, so the result over the decades has almost always been excellent racing.**

FERRARI 308GTB

Successor to the Dino, the first 308 was presented by the Italians in 1973 at the Paris show, and caused something of a stir. It was rare for a Ferrari not to be designed by Pininfarina and it was rare for Ferrari to use a V8 engine.

The body was by Bertone, and was a beautiful pattern of curves, getting a lot of car into a small space. The original twin-distributor 255 bhp engine was fitted transversely in the rear, with its cylinders quite close to each other because of the side-to-side space restrictions of the transverse engine. The car was not initially an outstanding success, and by 1975 had evolved into the Pininfarina-styled 308GTB, a two-seater with a strong family resemblance to the original Dino and the Boxer.

The 308 remained in production through the 1970s and the 1980s, running into trouble occasionally as emission controls became tighter. Fuel injection replaced the Webers, and the *Quattrovalvole* version of the car featured quad cams and four valves per cylinder, and power went back up to a respectable 240 bhp, with a top speed of a more than respectable 150mph (240kph).

Never the most outrageously styled Ferrari, the 308 was subtle and relatively restrained in appearance, although still beautiful in its own way – impressive without straining too hard.

FERRARI 308GTB 1973–85

BODY/CHASSIS Tubular steel framework with steel two-seater coupé body.

ENGINE Rear-mid mounted light alloy transverse V8, four valves per cylinder, quad cams, Bosch K-Jetronic fuel injection. 240 bhp at 7000 rpm.

TRANSMISSION Five-speed gearbox and transaxle, integral with sump casting, limited slip differential.

SUSPENSION Front: double wishbones, coil springs, telescopic shocks, anti-roll bar. Rear: double wishbones, coil springs, telescopic shocks, anti-roll bar.

34

Below: **With an all-alloy 3 litre quad-cam rear-mid mounted V8, a decent chassis and a sensible sized wheelbase and track, the 308 was one of the most practical supercars of its time, and could be hustled round tight country roads at astonishing speeds.**

Right: **The noise of a 3 litre Ferrari V8 engine being given a little room is enough to raise the hairs on most people's necks, driving it or just watching it hurtle past in a red blur. The earlier Bertone-styled 308GT4 had been Ferrari's first roadgoing V8. But nobody liked the style.**

Below: **Of the mid-engined Ferraris that preceded and followed the 308GTB, none quite captured its clean, balanced lines. Those flying buttresses would be seen on the Testarossa and today's 512TR.**

FORD MUSTANG

One of the great automotive success stories of all time, the US Ford Mustang was simple in concept – standard family car parts recycled within a sports body and a list of options longer than Sunset Strip. The original engine options included a 170 cubic inch (28 cubic metre) straight six for the shopping market, a 289CI V8 for the more enthusiastic driver, and a 428CI V8 for those who just didn't care.

The Mustang was not really designed with any serious sports performance in mind. The suspension was double wishbone at the front, which can certainly be made to handle reasonably well, but at the back it was still a live axle on cart springs, requiring considerable modification to stop the axle bouncing about like a bag of monkeys every time any serious power was applied.

The Mustang gave everyone exactly what they wanted in terms of price and specification. The base price was $2,368, which meant everyone thought it was a bargain and then happily spent about another $1,000 in options: 100,000 were sold in the first four months of production.

The following generation got wider and heavier, but the engine options included

additional power to balance this up. Carroll Shelby's GT350 Mustangs and the mighty Boss Mustangs preserved the sporting image of the car, even through the bloated Mach I period, and a Shelby Mustang was a serious high-performance car. It had modified suspension with Koni shocks, a large anti-roll bar, a Hi-Po 271 bhp 289 V8 further modified with a big carb, free-flow exhausts and other subtle modifications to take it to a genuine 306 bhp. The race version ran about 350 bhp. It looked as though this process would go on for ever, until the oil crisis and the feeble and ugly Mustang II.

Above: **There are a lot less corners in America than there are in Europe, and the Mustang looked like a sports car while remaining a practical four-seater, which was the key to its success. This is the Shelby GT350.**

Above: **Engine options went from a "cooking" straight six to 7 litre firebreathing monsters. The launch of the Mustang and its many options has to rank as one of the greatest marketing coups of all time.**

Right: **Carroll Shelby's GT350 was a seriously fast car. His motto: "too much is just right."**

Left: **Lee Iacocca had been under pressure from enthusiasts to bring back the two-seater Thunderbird for some time, but the idea evolved into something more practical and more saleable – the Mustang.**

FORD MUSTANG 1964–

🜨 **BODY/CHASSIS** Monocoque body/chassis unit, in convertible, coupé and hard top forms.

🜨 **ENGINE** Cast iron 170cu in straight six, cast iron 289cu in V8, 302cu in V8, 427cu in V8, 428cu in V8.

🜨 **TRANSMISSION** Three- or four-speed manual or automatic. Later four-speed manual. Live axle.

🜨 **SUSPENSION** Front: double wishbones with coil springs and telescopic shocks, anti-roll bars optional. Rear: leaf springs with telescopic shocks.

FORD THUNDERBIRD

The go-ahead for the Thunderbird project was given in February 1953. A year later a mock-up appeared at the Detroit Auto Show, and production began later that year.

The car was up against Chevrolet's Corvette, which was regarded by Ford people as an uncouth machine. Their reply to the Corvette would be more upmarket and would combine power and luxury. In the event, the Thunderbird was surprisingly restrained, and in comparison with its contemporaries, was a paragon of good taste – so long as you didn't fit the Continental Kit, which meant an external rear mounted spare wheel with twin chrome fake rockets.

Left: **The interior was designed to be upmarket of the Corvette, and was very comfortable. The crisply designed two-seater was to be abandoned in favour of four seats after just a few years. Ford were right: they sold a lot more.**

Ninety per cent of Thunderbird customers also bought the hard top that went with the car, and which featured a circular porthole instead of rear quarter windows.

The performance of the Thunderbird was respectable by the standards of the day: the original 290CI V8 produced nearly 200 bhp, and ran through a three-speed manual transmission with an overdrive unit. However, despite good weight distribution,

Left: **The Thunderbird's clean and elegant lines were something of a surprise at a time when US stylists were at their most excessive in terms of flamboyant shape and chrome. The Thunderbird actually offered more performance than the Chevrolet Corvette.**

FORD THUNDERBIRD 1954–

✦ **BODY/CHASSIS** Twin rail cross-braced ladder chassis with steel convertible two-door bodywork and GRP hardtop.

✦ **ENGINE** Early models: 290cu in cast iron V8, with four-barrel Ford/Holley carb and 198 bhp.

✦ **TRANSMISSION** Three-speed manual gearbox with overdrive, or three-speed automatic. Live axle.

✦ **SUSPENSION** Front: double wishbones and coil springs. Rear: leaf springs.

the handling was more family car than sports car, and after an early racetrack humiliation at the hands of a couple of Jaguar XK120s, the idea of Thunderbirds in competition was quietly dropped.

Later versions of the car became fatter and softer, as seems inevitable with most sporting car designs, and the Thunderbird sports idea rather faded with the introduction of four-seater versions.

Right: **The styling of the original Thunderbirds made enough of an impression within Ford to reappear in the British MkII Consul/Zephyr/ Zodiac series cars, and later Thunderbird styling cues surfaced in Britain in the Corsair.**

THE GHIA CONNECTION

Although the Italian styling houses have made their influence felt far and wide, Carrozzeria Ghia, founded in 1915 by Giacinto Ghia, was responsible for some of the most popular sports cars in Europe in the 1960s and 1970s. Following the Italian fashion for supplying chassis to coachbuilders for bodying, Ghia made many very attractive coupé bodies for Alfa Romeo, styled the Maserati Ghibli and were involved in projects for Rolls-Royce, Ford and Chrysler. They were also responsible for the unfortunate Mustang II.

The first car which brought the name Ghia to the attention of the general public was the Volkswagen Beetle-based Karmann Ghia. This was a sports car very much in the MG mould, with fairly standard mechanicals and a pretty body. Very pretty, in fact,

Above and right: **As with so many classic sports cars, the Ghia's lovely curves concealed a prosaic floorpan, in this case that of the Beetle.**

with a long, sporty nose effectively conceal-ing the fact that there was still a Beetle engine in the back.

The Karmann Ghia's sweeping, curved steel bodywork was constructed by Karmann in Germany, and unfortunately contained a good number of rust traps. The car is thus as popular among restorers, who make a good living out of patching them back together, as it is among VW enthusiasts. There was a later and more modern version of the Karmann Ghia, which was less of a success than the earlier plump and curvy version.

One of Ghia's other big successes was the updating of Michelotti's Triumph TR5 into the TR6. This was an extremely difficult exercise, not least because production tool-ing was required 14 months after the contract was signed. Also, the TR5 was a handsome car, with excellent proportions, and it is easy indeed to throw the good away

with the bad when asked to update a now tired but once perfectly acceptable design.

Ghia left the centre and sides of the car more or less alone, which was wise, and got rid of all the chrome jewellery. They then moved the headlights out to the extremes of the grille aperture and smoothed out the line of the bonnet, getting rid of the vesti-gial power bulge left over from the 1950s. The small upright lamps faired in to the wings in the back end were changed and the body lines were essentially allowed to run straight back and then cut off sharply, with a large, modern set of rear lamps running

across the back and spilling round the sides (which also helped comply with transat-lantic side-light regulations). The car became sharper, more aggressive and much more modern in character, and continued to sell well on both sides of the Atlantic.

Having successfully made the "soft" Karmann Ghia and the "tough" TR6, Ghia were absorbed by Ford. This resulted in the De Tomaso Pantera and the RS200 rally car. The name of Ghia, however, has been so devalued by Ford's marketing that it now means little more than imitation wood trim on the more expensive Granadas; a not uncommon fate for a great name. The Triumph name itself, for example, was used on the Honda-Ballade-based Acclaim saloon for no particularly good reason at all.

Below left and right: **The fashionably sharp 1970s lines clearly influenced Ghia's restyling of the big Triumph.**

41

JAGUAR E-TYPE

The E-Type evolved from the D-Type, but while the D-Type could be accused of looking rather curtailed, particularly in short-nose form, the shape of the E-Type was sublime. Designed by Malcolm Sayer with the active involvement of Jaguar boss William Lyons, the proportions of the car were just about perfect.

Right: **Even if Jaguar's performance figures were on the optimistic side, the E-Type was still very, very fast and represented an astonishing amount of car for the money.**

Above: **The 3.8 litre version of the XK engine that was originally fitted to the E-Type was said to produce 265 bhp with triple SU carbs, and to power the car to a top speed of 150mph (240kph).**

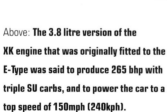

The construction of the car followed the same ideas that had been successfully tried out on its predecessor – the rear part of the car was a complicated monococque and the front end was a tracery of tubing, which

Below: **When looking at the E-Type, it is easy to forget that it had the same engine as the XK150, a powerplant from 1948.**

JAGUAR E-TYPE 1961–75

✦ **BODY/CHASSIS** Steel monococque coupé and convertible body/chassis units, with tubular front chassis and flip-up steel front end.

✦ **ENGINE** 3.8 litre straight six double overhead cam, with triple SU carbs. Later 4.2 litre and 5.3 litre V12 options.

✦ **TRANSMISSION** Four-speed manual gearbox with overdrive and automatic options. Fixed limited-slip diff with independent driveshafts.

✦ **SUSPENSION** Front: double wishbones with torsion bars and telescopic shocks. Rear: suspension cage located by bushes and front locating arms; four coil-over shocks.

43

supported the front suspension and the by now legendary double overhead cam six-cylinder XK engine.

The suspension and drivetrain had moved away from live axles and were becoming relatively sophisticated. The back suspension assembly was remotely mounted on a subframe, making the cabin a very civilized place. The suspension was independent at the front and rear, with fixed length driveshafts used as wishbones, and disc brakes all round, inboard at the rear.

Right: Like the XK120, it was difficult to decide whether the coupé or the convertible was prettier. The V12 engine would give the E-Type a final incarnation.

JAGUAR XK120/140

The Jaguar XK120 was designed mainly to show off the brand new XK series double overhead cam engine of 1948, and rumour has it that the first XK120 was conceived and constructed in two weeks. The design suggests this is true – there is no hint of compromise in what must be one of the purest automotive shapes ever to go into production. Certainly if the accountants had had a say, they would have objected to the idea of a pure two-seater with very little luggage space that was well over 14 feet (4.3 metres) long.

The basis of the car was a shortened MkVII chassis, and everything but the brakes proved to be well up to the performance of the engine. The 120 referred to the expected top speed of the car and was regarded with some suspicion, as 120mph (192kph) was a respectable speed for a racing car in 1948. However, on a journalistic jamboree to Jabbeke in Belgium, the British press saw an XK top 130 mph (208kph).

There was to be an XK100, with a four-cylinder engine, but Jaguar were swamped

Below: **Despite the brakes, the XK120 did very well in competition, winning the Alpine Rally in the hands of Ian Appleyard, the Tourist Trophy in the hands of Stirling Moss and finally Le Mans in spaceframe C-type form.**

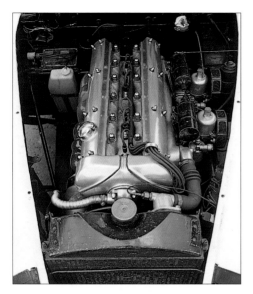

Above: **The legendary double overhead cam straight six powered Jaguars for nearly 40 years.**

JAGUAR XK120/140 1948–57

⚙ **BODY/CHASSIS** Twin rail cross-braced steel ladder chassis, with aluminium and later steel convertible and coupé bodywork.

⚙ **ENGINE** 3.4 litre straight six double overhead cam, cast iron with alloy head. Two SU carbs.

⚙ **TRANSMISSION** Four-speed manual gearbox, live axle.

⚙ **SUSPENSION** Front: double wishbones with torsion bars and lever arm shocks. Rear: leaf springs with lever arm shocks.

with orders for the six-cylinder car, and the four was never made.

The handling was very good by the standards of the time, and the levels of equipment and comfort, particularly in the coupé form, were high, with an abundance of leather and wood. The hard top is as beautiful as the open top sports, and the body shape turned out to be not only gorgeous but aerodynamically very effective.

The drum brakes were not quite up to the demands of a 130mph (208kph) car, and many people had a nasty shock when they discovered that the XK's brakes didn't quite match the power and the handling.

Right: **The later XK140 remained basically true to the original XK shape, adding hefty bumpers in place of the original delicate flutes, and the weight began to creep up.**

LAMBORGHINI MIURA

If ever a Lamborghini could be called subtle, this would be the one. Italian sports car styling of the early 1970s was not noted for restraint, but the Miura was relatively understated, certainly by comparison with the later and rather grotesque Countach.

The gearbox was under and behind the engine, and the differential was directly driven from the gearbox. That meant the whole installation, located right behind the driver's shoulder, could be hidden behind the flying buttresses that topped the curvy rear wing, and the proportions of the car remained beautifully balanced. It also

Right: **The Miura avoided the usual tendency for rear-engined supercars to look tail-heavy, by the simple but radical expedient of locating the Lamborghini-built V12 engine transversely, across the chassis.**

LAMBORGHINI MIURA 1967–71

⊛ **BODY/CHASSIS** Sheet steel monocoque substructure with alloy body panels over.

⊛ **ENGINE** Transverse V12 of 3929cc, with 4 overhead cams and 4 triple Weber 40IDL carburettors, producing 385 bhp at 7,000 rpm.

⊛ **TRANSMISSION** Five-speed manual gearbox in unit with engine casting. Limited slip differential directly driven from gearbox.

⊛ **SUSPENSION** Front: double wishbones with coil-over shocks and anti-roll bar. Rear: double wishbones and coil-over shocks with high level anti-roll bar.

Left: **Although beautifully appointed and very comfortable, the cockpit became a sauna in hot weather.**

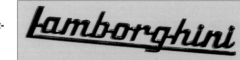

meant that the noises from 12 air intakes, 4 cam chains, 24 thrashing valves and the sound emitted from the ends of the complicated tangle of exhaust pipes were all unusually close to your ears – despite a thick aluminium bulkhead and glass window, a Miura is not a quiet place to be. Still, if you didn't like listening to that sort of music, you wouldn't be driving that sort of car.

With an undisputed bhp figure of 385 in Super Veloce form and the ideal weight distribution matched by good suspension design, the relatively small Miura could provide extremely fast cross-country progress.

Luggage capacity was laughable and the pop-up headlights weren't much use at high speeds – but Ferruccio Lamborghini shrugged his shoulders at the former, and suggested that nights could be more enjoyably spent elsewhere than in a motor car.

Left: **The pop-up head-lights were not very effective. Fast cars need commensurately powerful lights.**

Right: **The Miura's top speed was somewhere between 177 and 190mph (283 and 304kph), depending on who was doing the telling. Where did Lamborghini first find success in the automotive world? Tractors!**

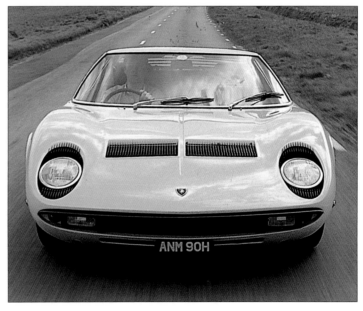

LOTUS ELAN

Colin Chapman achieved racing success by removing every last fraction of weight from his cars and by tuning small engines to the maximum. He thought that a successful racing car should be strong enough to win, but that much more strength than that would be wasted. His long line of Lotus Sevens consisted of not much more than a skinned spaceframe and an engine, and the cars are still being copied at the rate of somewhere between 50 and 100 a week.

However, the Elan represented a slightly different approach, and provided such unheard-of luxuries as windows and a roof.

The interior featured a wood-veneered dashboard, and was very well equipped, even luxurious. Chapman's technique of using soft, small diameter road springs, intended originally to keep the wheels in contact with the track at all times, had the beneficial side-effect of providing a very comfortable ride.

The car was still as light as possible, though, and the chassis was remarkable. A

sheet steel backbone with forks at either end upon which to hang the engine and suspension meant it was six times as

Below: **As happens frequently when an object is designed with function uppermost, the Elan was one of the prettiest sports cars of the 1960s, with excellent proportions despite its diminutive size.**

Above: **The engine, mounted well back in the chassis for good weight distribution, was based on the bottom half of Ford's ubiquitous four-cylinder Cortina unit.**

LOTUS ELAN 1962–74

⊛ **BODY/CHASSIS** Perforated sheet steel backbone, with unstressed GRP convertible and coupé bodywork.

⊛ **ENGINE** Double overhead cam version of Ford 116E four-cylinder, with twin side-draught Webers, producing 100 bhp.

⊛ **TRANSMISSION** Four-speed manual gearbox, fixed differential with optional final drive ratios.

⊛ **SUSPENSION** Front: double wishbone with coil-over shocks and anti-roll bar. Rear: struts with coil-over shocks and A-frames.

stiff as earlier Lotus GP spaceframes, and weighed 75 pounds (34 kilograms).

The Elan's Cortina-based engine was fitted with a Lotus-designed light alloy twin-cam cylinder head and two fat Webers.

The result of that was to up the engine's output to 100 bhp and to cut its weight at the same time.

The suspension relied on long travel and light springs, and the independent rear end consisted of struts with coil-over shocks, and A-frames running forwards to locate the Rotoflex-equipped driveshafts. Elegant and very effective.

Left: **The bodywork was of unitary construction in GRP and didn't contribute to the stiffness of the chassis – at least until the latter rusted.**

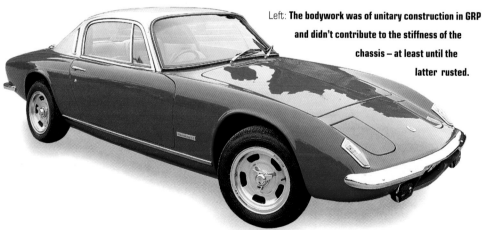

49

RALLY MILESTONES

Make no mistake, front wheel drive only exists because it is cheap and easy to make, and because it makes a usefully compact package for small, everyday cars. Almost without exception, cars that are any fun are rear wheel drive, with the one notable exception of the Mini, and in particular the Mini Cooper.

The Mini is enormous fun to drive and can be thrown about more or less at will. There is a wheel at each corner, the centre of gravity is low and the amount of grip remarkable. In addition, the overall tiny proportions of the car and the fact that you are only just above the ground makes the car feel very much like a kart.

The Mini Cooper was developed by John Cooper, who saw the potential in the Mini before nearly everyone else, and who improved the power, the brakes and the tyre widths to make the Mini do what it already did very well, but even more competently. The Mini Cooper S, the ultimate Cooper, more or less took over various forms of motorsport, and the French at one stage had to resort to disqualifying Minis for having "over-bright headlights" in order to stop a complete British whitewash.

Part of the success of the Mini was psychological – you felt you could get away with anything in a Mini, and if you went into a competition with that attitude you were on to a winner before you started. Particularly if the car was capable of delivering the promises you were making on its behalf every time you hurtled into a snowy corner 30mph (48kph) too fast.

Another rally success is the Audi Quattro, one of very few cars that were

Above: **The Mini Cooper was so successful in its early rallying career that the French authorities banned it for having incorrect headlights! John Cooper is still producing Mini specials today.**

Above: **A Cooper makes an excellent practical classic, but check the history of any example extremely carefully: a lot are fakes. The Cooper company earned a royalty on cars bearing their name: in 1971, about £2 ($4)!**

worth bothering about throughout the 1980s. The Quattro was the first practical four-wheel drive high-speed sports car, and it redefined the concept of grip.

The ground-breaking Quattro merged the successful Audi 80 and the earlier 1960s Ferguson Formula 4WD ideas as used on the Jensen Interceptor FF. It didn't take long for rally driving daredevils to discover the potential, and before any time at all had passed, the Quattro was a world rally champion. The victorious works rally cars were achieving something very close to 500 bhp.

The acceleration of the straightforward road cars, with 300 bhp available and total grip, is astonishing, and the 0–60 (0–96) times are under five seconds. Mind you, for most people the Quattro is less than entirely practical as a daily classic – a replacement gearbox costs rather more than a brand new shopping car – though rust is not normally

a problem. The non-turbocharged five-cylinder Audi 80 Coupé with four wheel drive but without the fat wheel arches is a car to buy right now – they will never be cheaper and are likely to become very valuable. The Quattro survived as late as 1991.

Above: **The Quattro's handling was simply incredible. If you were foolish enough to try it, roundabouts could be taken at 70mph (112kph).**

Below: **Off-road, the Quattro redefined the parameters of the rally car.**

MGB CHROME BUMPER

The MGB followed the inevitable sports car route to becoming bigger and softer than its elegant predecessor the MGA, but in so doing became one of the most popular sports cars ever, selling in total over 500,000 units during its production life. The car was more of a tourer than a sports car in character, and when looked at in that light, its modest performance and handling abilities don't look so inadequate.

Low on power but reasonable on torque, the long-stroke four made lovely bear-like noises and loped happily across country at touring speeds.

A GT version was inevitable and the higher windscreen line and roof of the BGT did no harm to the car's looks. The roof stiffened the already quite solid chassis, and the coupé body provided a genuinely useful amount of luggage space and even a vestigial rear seat for very small people.

Below: **Pretty, understated styling made the MGB a worldwide favourite among sports car enthusiasts.**

Right: **The MGB has a low centre of gravity and is strong – fit decent suspension and power for some weekend competition on the racetrack.**

The MGC, fitted with the Austin Westminster/Healey straight six, was intended to fill the gap in the market left by the Austin-Healey 3000, but didn't.

A Rover V8 powered version of the MGB provided 137 bhp compared to the original 95 bhp, but hauling the hefty chassis about was still quite hard work, and the top speed of 125mph (200kph) and the 0–60 (0–96) of 8.2 seconds were still quite leisurely, although the inelegantly named MGB GTV8 made even better growling noises than the B-engined variants.

The handsome proportions of the car were virtually ruined in the early 1970s in order to comply with American ride-height requirements. The car was perched a little higher and fitted with huge and unsightly plastic bumpers. With all its faults, however, the MGB is still a well-loved and very attractive car that maintains an enthusiastic following worldwide.

Right: **The MGB's mechanical base was the venerable Morris Oxford/Austin Cambridge, with the 1600cc B-series engine bored out to the maximum 1800cc and equipped with an extra carb.**

MGB CHROME BUMPER 1962–74

⚙ **BODY/CHASSIS** Pressed steel monocoque shell, in convertible and coupé versions.

⚙ **ENGINE** 1798cc four-cylinder all cast iron B-series, with cam in block. Two SU carburettors. Later, 3 litre straight six, and light alloy Rover V8 options.

⚙ **TRANSMISSION** Four-speed manual gearbox, with synchro on three gears. Later all synchro. Limited number of automatic models made. Live axle.

⚙ **SUSPENSION** Front: torsion bar, telescopic shocks, anti-roll bar. Rear: leaf springs, lever arm shocks.

53

MORGAN ROADSTER

M organ's waiting list is as long as its history, which goes back to 1935 with more or less the same model. The car still has cart springs at the back and sliding pillar suspension at the front, which most people regarded as old-fashioned when biplanes were current. Morgan steadfastly refuse to change, and the queue of customers suggests that their complete lack of product planning suits them and their buyers just fine.

The construction of a contemporary Plus 8 is still pretty much the same as the first Morgan four-wheeler of 1935, with a simple steel chassis and a body constructed with coachbuilding technology from a bent ash frame with aluminium stretched over it. This gives one decided benefit for the long-term owner in that you can still get panels for any Morgan; and considering the skill and effort that goes into making them, they are remarkably cheap.

Morgan have never made their own engines, and have simply bought whatever seemed a good engine from the major manufacturers of the time. Hence, the first three-wheeled Morgans had JAP motorbike engines, and through the first 50 years of the four-wheeled Morgan's life it ran on Ford, Coventry Climax, Standard, Triumph, Ford again, and finally Rover V8 and Ford straight four.

Above: **The V8 Morgan's 0–60 (0–96) time of 6.1 seconds will still frighten most current "fast" cars – so as far as Morgan are concerned,** *plus ça change.*

Left: **The handling of the 60-year-old design, with a light overall weight, a powerful Rover V8 and fat, low-profile modern tyres, is still superb.**

Right: **The limited-move-ment sliding pillar front suspension, while provid-ing a boneshaking ride, keeps the wheels very flat on the road, to great effect. The best buy? Brand new – if you can stand the wait, that is.**

MORGAN ROADSTER 1935–

◈ **CHASSIS/BODY** Twin rail ladder frame, with ash framed steel and aluminium bodywork.

◈ **ENGINE** Currently Rover V8 of 3532cc, with fuel injection, and four-cylinder Ford engines.

◈ **TRANSMISSION** Rover five-speed manual gearbox, live axle.

◈ **SUSPENSION** Front: sliding pillar with coil springs. Rear: leaf springs.

PORSCHE – BEETLE TO 911

The first Porsches to come out of Germany were similar to the Karmann Ghia concept: pretty, sporty bodywork on the Volkswagen Beetle floorpan. They were very appealing if not exactly handsome, with fat little pudding-basin bodywork. But, while the Karmann approach continued to rely on charm, the Porsche began to go faster. It was still based on VW parts, but increasingly they were tweaked before being fitted, and Porsche versions of the Beetle's air-cooled flat four continued to develop from the fairly feeble original. The 356, particularly in Speedster form with a cut-down, minimalist windscreen, is a delight to drive. The steering is feather-light, the engine enthusiastic and the handling – up to a point – is nimble and sharp. Both the front and back suspension are by torsion bar, and the rear drive is via swing half-axles, but the axles aren't a problem, as they are on a Triumph. The only handling defect in the Porsche is that the engine is hanging out way behind the rear axle, so when the tail end slides, it does so in earnest, and you have to know what you are doing to recover it.

Although the engine noise can be tiring on long journeys, there is a lot of room to stretch out, and with all the storage space and odd nooks and crannies there is plenty of room for a holiday's worth of luggage.

The 356 evolved into the 911, which became one of the all-time desirable fast cars. Unfortunately, it was hijacked during

Above: **The early coupé shape is quite beautiful for a rear-engined car. But be warned if you are tempted: they rust horribly.**

Above: **Those early convertibles are really coveted today, though they never had anything like what is now Porsche performance.**

the 1980s by bond dealers with no style and money to waste, and before long they became rather unfashionable. However, as the memories of the 1980s gradually fade, the Porsche brand is becoming socially rehabilitated again.

The Porsche 911 was still recognizably the descendant of the Beetle, and even the engine fitted to the RS Carrera, a 3 litre aircooled flat six kicking out more than 200 bhp, was still a development of the old Volkswagen flat four.

There is still a current version of the car, which to Porsche's credit has not gone the way of all sports cars to become fat and slow as the generations continue. The 911 has certainly got fatter, but only because the wheel arches have bulged out ever further, not to make room for comfortable seats for an ageing clientele. Later versions of the 911 had bigger and bigger rear wheels, and the engine hanging out over the axle certainly

gives excellent initial grip, but it is wise to bear in mind that if you are hooligan enough to provoke a 911 into letting go, it will turn and bite you with more venom than a Cobra. A short wheel base, rear-wheel drive and weight at the back mean trouble.

Above: **Over the years, the little pudding bowl got more and more powerful. The latest Le Mans-derived GT1 road car is petrifyingly fast.**

Below: **Do not provoke a tail slide in a 911 unless you really know what you are doing.**

RELIANT SCIMITAR GTE

The Reliant Scimitar was the first ever GT estate and represented a whole new class of car. It was also basically a very good car. However, perhaps because of the negligible credibility of the Reliant company brought about by the introduction of the Robin three-wheeler, the Scimitar has always been a very underrated sports car. Looked at rationally, it has to offer the best value for money of any sporting classic. The car has a competent and solid chassis, a rust-free GRP body and a very well-ordered undercarriage. The front suspension is Triumph TR6, and the rear end is Ford; but instead of the cheap and cheerful leaf spring set-up, the Reliant has a four-bar rear end, with long enough bars to ensure good vertical axle location. It also has a Watts linkage for sideways axle location – which is one better than a Panhard rod and correspondingly more expensive. Ford's Essex V6,

Right: **The original paint colour options were unusual. The SE5A (shown here), introduced in 1971, has the uprated engine with 138bhp.**

uprated for the SE5A, provides plenty of power for a light car.

The Ford V6 is quite heavy and relies on torque rather than bhp. If the fibre timing wheel is replaced by a steel one and the oil pump drive is renewed every so often, the engine will run for ever. In the Scimitar, the front-mounted spare wheel obstructs airflow to the radiator, making cooling marginal if the radiator is not in top condition. However, as a good Scimitar is half the price of an MGB, a new radiator now and then is a small price to pay.

RELIANT SCIMITAR GTE 1968–86

⚘ **CHASSIS/BODY** Twin rail ladder chassis, with GRP sports estate bodyshell, later convertible.

⚘ **ENGINE** Ford Essex cast iron 3 litre V6, 128 bhp (SE5) then 138bhp (SE5A).

⚘ **TRANSMISSION** Four-speed Ford gearbox with optional overdrive, or three-speed automatic. Live axle.

⚘ **SUSPENSION** Front: double wishbone with coil-over shocks, anti-roll bar. Rear: four-bar set-up with Watts linkage.

Left: **The interior is very comfortable and well equipped, and the 2 + 2 seating readily converts into a small and still attractive estate car.**

59

Right: **The Scimitar is so undervalued that even when you add the cost of a decent respray in something like silver or British racing green, it's still a bargain.**

RENAULT ALPINE

The Renault Alpine was born in France in 1955, when rally driver Jean Redélé built a small coupé based on the mechanics of the Renault 4CV. From that grew the little Alpine organization closely linked with Renault, which was in fact bought by the latter in 1974.

From the start, the car featured the basic design principles of rear engine and drive, with a tubular backbone chassis and plastic bodywork. The suspension featured well-controlled swing axles at the back and anti-roll bars front and rear. In general, engines remained below 1700cc, although Amédée Gordini did build a 3 litre V8 for a Le Mans version of the car.

The squat rear end with its exaggerated negative camber was partly to compensate for the weight of the engine overhanging at the back by placing the tyres flat on the road at the extremes of cornering, and partly to discourage the swing axles from jacking up under provocation – a terrifying feature shared with the Triumph Herald.

The A108 Alpine evolved into the A310, retaining the tubular backbone and hotted-up rear mounted Renault engines, but a new, sleek body changed the look of the car. In the mid-1970s the slick V6, more usually employed to power the Renault 25 and various Volvos and Peugeots, was squeezed into the Alpine's engine bay, still hanging right

Above: **The Renault Alpine developed from a more or less pure competition car into a sports racer.**

Right: **This 1970s Alpine interior is proposeful if a little dated in style terms.**

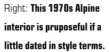

Right: **The Michelotti-inspired design of the Alpine A110, which appeared in 1963, was true to Redélé's concept. It had approximately 750 Renault parts in every car – are those Citroën Dyane front indicators?**

Below: **On the edge, an Alpine was a handful and would provide a spectacular sideways display for any spectators, which made it very popular among French rally drivers.**

Below: **Engine sizes grew from 956 to 1951 for the Alpine A110.**

61

out at the back. Despite mounting everything that weighs anything – fuel tank, battery and so on – right in the nose, to balance the weight, the car required even more skill than before to drive quickly. With 205/70 section rear tyres, it would hang on grimly through a very fast corner, but when it let go, it would do so in fine style.

The model designations of the Alpine are legion; make sure you know what you are looking at if you ever intend to buy.

RENAULT ALPINE 1955–95

🜨 **CHASSIS/BODY** Tubular backbone integral with plastic bodyshell.

🜨 **ENGINE** Various rear-mounted Renault engines including several four-cylinders and the 2.6 litre V6.

🜨 **TRANSMISSION** Four- and five-speed manual gearboxes, rear wheel drive.

🜨 **SUSPENSION** Front: upper and lower control arms, coil springs. Rear: trailing radius arms and swing arms.

FUTURE CLASSICS

Although it is difficult to predict which contemporary cars will become the classics of the future, there are some that certainly should be considered.

Jaguar have produced a long string of successful and charismatic sports cars, starting with the SS100 and continuing with the XK and the E-Type. The XJS, although it had the ingredients, never caught the imagination. The new XK8, however, has fulfilled

Above: **The XK8's cabin is fashionably further forward than earlier Jaguar sports cars', but the proportions are still fine. To take an example of attention to detail: for most cars, cross members are mild steel and welded, for the XK8 they are cast in aluminium and machine finished.**

Left: **The XK8 is already Jaguar's best-selling sports car of all time. The floorpan is modified from the XJS.**

Below: **Jaguar's new V8 may be slightly muffled by the catalytic convertors, but it still sounds wonderful.**

its destiny. The performance and the reliability don't really matter: the car has successfully taken the best of Jaguar's styling cues from the 1950s and 1960s and has blended nostalgia with a very effective and dramatic 1990s shape. The body is a little too long and the bonnet a bit short for perfect front-engined sports car proportions, but every other coupé these days is that shape, and to go too retro would probably have been a mistake. The E-Type was one of Jaguar's all-time best in terms of styling and character and the bonnet of the XK8 features the same radiator aperture and central bonnet bulge: all that's missing is the length.

Inside, the XK8 continues the Jaguar tradition of leather-bound opulence, with a choice of colours varying from luxurious to vulgar. Prices, although not as remarkably low as they were for Jaguars of yesteryear, are still sensible and offer good value.

The TVR Griffith, and its stablemates the Chimaera and the Cerbera, represent current thinking at TVR. Griffith is a name that goes back into TVR's fractious and uneven history – the first car to bear the name was a small sports car with a tubular backbone spaceframe, with a big American V8 stuffed into the engine bay.

Below: **TVR claim well over 150mph (240kph) for their Griffith and Chimaera supercars, and there is no reason to doubt them.**

The Griffith of today is a slightly bigger tubular backbone spaceframe sports car, which has TVR's own race-developed V8 fitted into the engine bay. It's not quite such an animal as the first generation Griffith, but it's still a proper sports car, not just a "sporting car". The cabin has changed dramatically from the early days, and is now a space-age collection of leather-bound swoops and curves, and the body has been cleared of all clutter; even the door handles have been reduced to buttons.

The convertible top is a model of elegant engineering, properly weatherproof, with a hard centre section that stows in the boot (trunk). The proportions are absolutely uncompromised, with the cabin at the rear, a large engine at the front and enough hand-made individuality to please even the most demanding of the next generation's classic car enthusiasts.

63

INDEX

ACKNOWLEDGEMENTS

The publishers would like to thank the following for supplying pictures: Haymarket Specialist Motoring for: p.8; p.9t; p.10t; p.14–15; p.16; p.18–19b; p.20; p.21t; p.23t; p.24; p.25tl+br; p.26–7; p.28; p.29tr; p.32; p.33bl; p.34; p.35bl+tr; p.36–7; p.39br; p.40–1; p.42tr; p.44; p.45tr+tl; p.46–53; p.54br; p.55b; p.56bl+br; p.57t; p.58-9; p.61; and p.63.
National Motor Museum, Beaulieu, England, for: p.6; p.7; p.9b; p.10b (N. Wright); p.11–13; p.17; p.18t (N. Wright); p.21b; p.22; p.23b; p.25bl; p.28tr (N. Wright); p.33t; p.38; p.42ml; p.43br (N. Wright); p.45br; p.54bl; p.55t; p.56t; p.57b (N. Wright); p.60 (N. Georgano); p.62t+bl.
Iain Ayre for: p.30–31.
The French Picture Library for: p.33br.
Andrew Moreland for: p.35br, p.42b; p.62br.

b=bottom; t=top; l=left; r=right; m=middle.